WESTMINSTER SCHOOLS

SMYTHE GAMBRELL
LIBRARY

PRESENTED BY

Anne E. Flinn

EVE SIBLEY

THE SEA LIBRARY | CORAL REEF FISH

by Sue Beauregard and Jill Fairchild

The Children's Book Company

28267

Consultant: Heidi Hahn
Scripps Institution of Oceanography

Photography by Carl Roessler: cover, 1, 2–3, 9, 10, 14, 21, 22,
25, 26, 29, 31; Stan Keiser: 4–5, 6, 13, 17;
Steinhart Aquarium and J. C. Hookelheim: 18.

Designed by Richard Crawford and David Mekelburg.

Published by Cypress Publishing Group,
Glendale, California 91204.
Distributed by The Children's Book Company,
Mankato, Minnesota 56001.
Printed in the United States of America.
Library of Congress Number: 77-71290
International Standard Book Number: 0-89813-021-2

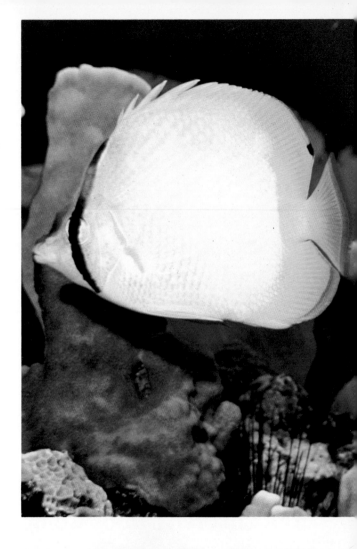

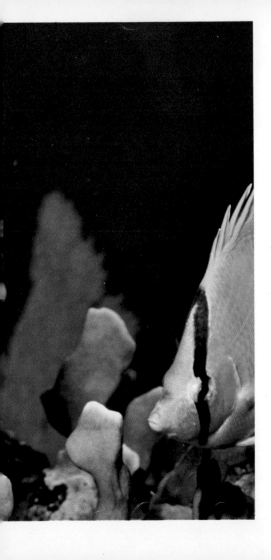

Put on your flippers, goggles, and snorkle and dive right in.

The coral reef is a beautiful place to be. You see life and color all around you.

The water is shallow. It is warmed by sun. Coral reefs are found only in warm tropical oceans. And so are the fish that live in these reefs.

Coral reef fish dart everywhere you look. Some of them are curious. They swim up to take a close look at you. That's great because now you can take a close look at them…

The parrot fish lives in the coral reef with millions of neighbors.

The coral reef is a great place for fish to live. There is plenty of food here and many places to hide.

Parrot fish have strong jaws. They grind up pieces of coral for food.

Corals are tiny animals called polyps. The coral polyps live attached to one another. Different kinds of corals grow in different shapes, sizes, and colors.

6

A graceful angelfish takes bites of food from nooks and crannies in the coral.

Most coral reef fish are small. Some coral reef fish swim alone. Some swim in pairs. Some swim in schools. When the fish are frightened, they all disappear into their hiding places in the reef.

Each fish stakes out a small area of the coral reef and makes that its homeplace.

Look for the small, yellow pointed spine near the mouth of this angelfish. All angelfish have a spine like that.

Here's another angelfish. Do you see the blue spine near its mouth? There are many varieties of angelfish. Each seems to be more beautiful than the other.

The colors of most coral reef fish are bright and beautiful. Nobody knows for certain why coral reef fish are so colorful. Maybe their colors give a message to other fish: I am here. This is my territory. Stay away.

9

These fish are butterfly fish. They are related to angelfish. From the side, butterflies and angels look round and fat. But from the front, they look as thin as a pancake.

The thin shape of these coral reef fish helps to protect them. When a larger fish comes near, they can dart into narrow openings in the coral. And they turn to face the danger head-on. From the front they're almost too thin to be noticed.

The black stripe across the eyes of these butterflies also helps protect them. The stripe breaks up their body shape and makes it difficult for another fish to tell which end is front.

The shiny barracuda is a fast swimmer with a big appetite. Barracudas swim slowly along the edge of the reef. They watch for small fish that stray from the protection of the reef. When a fish comes along, the barracuda moves with lightning speed to catch a meal.

This lovely, bright fish is called a grouper. But that doesn't mean it swims in groups. The grouper swims alone.

There are many kinds of groupers. They come in all sizes. This grouper is only 25 centimeters long.

All fish have fins. They use their fins to move through water and to balance, steer, and brake. Different kinds of fish have different shaped fins. The skin of fish is usually covered by scales.

Fish can live only in water. They breathe by taking in water through their mouths. There is oxygen in water. The water passes out through gills on each side of their heads. The gills take the oxygen from the water. You can see the gill cover on the side of this grouper.

Some groupers grow so large they weigh hundreds of kilograms, like this one.

Groupers eat small coral reef fish. Maybe the grouper should be called a gulper. It opens its big mouth wide and sucks in a meal.

18

The dragon moray eel looks fierce. But it's really shy. Like all fish it opens its mouth to breathe.

Moray eels stay In their hiding places during the day. They come out at night to hunt. They have a long, thin shape that lets them slither into the hiding places of other animals.

Look at the moray eel's sharp teeth. The teeth point backward toward its mouth. When the moray eel snaps its mouth shut on an animal, there is no escape.

The green moray eel uses its "nose" to find food. Moray eels don't see very well, but they have a keen sense of smell. Their tube-shaped nostrils are unusual and very helpful. The nostrils can work separately to pick up the scents of animals in different places. Moray eels will eat almost any fish.

22

Some fish help each other. This tiny cleaner wrasse is eating parasites living on the skin of a larger wrasse. The cleaner wrasse gets a meal. The larger wrasse gets rid of those parasites.

Cleaner wrasses sometimes have all kinds of coral reef fish lined up and waiting to be worked on. Large fish let the cleaners enter their mouths without eating them. The cleaners are important to the health of coral reef fish. If there are no cleaner fish in an area, there will probably be no other fish living there either.

The clownfish lives among the stinging tentacles of a sea anemone.

Anemones are animals. They fasten themselves to rocks and usually stay in one place. They wait for small fish to bump against their stinging tentacles. The sting paralyzes the fish.

But the sting of an anemone doesn't hurt clownfish. A mucus covers the body of the clownfish. It protects the clownfish from the poison.

The clownfish and the anemone have a partnership. The clownfish brings food to the anemone. Any fish that tries to catch a clownfish will probably become a meal for the anemone. And the anemone keeps the clownfish safe.

25

Young fish are called fry.

The young of most coral reef fish don't look like their parents. Their color and shape are different.

Fish usually lay large numbers of small eggs and leave them. But clownfish and some other coral reef fish guard their eggs until they hatch. As soon as they hatch, the young are on their own. Small fry swim together in schools for several weeks. Many are eaten by larger fish.

The seahorse looks like a tiny armored horse. But it's a fish.

Seahorses eat tiny drifting animals. They also eat tiny fish just hatched from eggs.

Seahorses are different from other fish in many ways. They swim in an upright position. They use their tails for holding onto plants and coral. But one of the most remarkable things about seahorses is the way they take care of their eggs. The female seahorse puts her eggs in a pouch in the belly of the male seahorse. The male carries the eggs in his pouch for about three weeks until they hatch. The young are about one centimeter long at birth. And they look just like their parents.

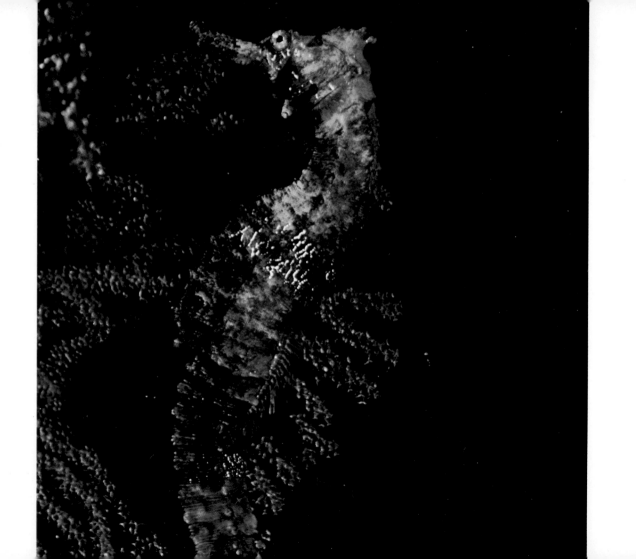

29

When the porcupine fish is frightened, it gulps in water. The water puffs the fish up like a big spiny ball. Its spines are so sharp not many fish will try to swallow it. When the fear is gone, the porcupine fish slowly lets the water out until its spines lie flat again.

In the coral reef, there are more kinds of fish with more colors, shapes, and patterns than anywhere in the whole wide water world.

Take a closer look: Name what you see here.
Match the photographs to the pictures inside your book.